P9-BJW-261

Persistence Will Pay

Never Stop.Never Quit.Persist.

By Avtar Garcha

Copyright © 2024 by Avtar Garcha

All rights reserved. No part of this book may be used or
reproduced by any means, graphic, electronic, or mechanical,
including photocopying, recording, taping, or by any
information storage retrieval system, without the written
permission of the publisher except in the case of brief quotations
embodied in critical articles and reviews.

ii

Contents

Introduction

I tried looking for the meaning of persistence in various dictionaries.

The best one I found in Vocubulary.com. Persistence is the act of continuing an activity without interruption. Best example is you try and try to learn some new skill and never give up.

In the pursuit of any worthwhile endeavor, from personal goals to professional aspirations, one quality stands out as indispensable: persistence. It is the relentless determination to keep pushing forward, despite setbacks, obstacles, and challenges. In this booklet, we delve into the essence of persistence, exploring its significance, understanding its underlying principles, and uncovering strategies to cultivate and harness its transformative power in our lives.

CHAPTER 1

Understanding Persistence

Persistence is more than just a willingness to keep going—it is a mindset, a way of life. In this chapter, we explore the essence of persistence, defining what it means to persist in the face of adversity. We delve into the psychology behind persistence, examining the traits and characteristics that differentiate those who persevere from those who give up.

Here are key aspects to consider:

Commitment to Goals: Persistence is fueled by a strong commitment to your goals. It involves setting clear objectives and staying dedicated to achieving them despite obstacles or setbacks. When you're committed to your goals, you're more likely to persevere through difficulties and maintain focus on the desired outcomes.

- **Resilience in the Face of Challenges**: Persistence requires resilience—the ability to bounce back from setbacks and adversity. It's natural to encounter obstacles and setbacks along the way, but what sets persistent individuals apart is their willingness to learn from failures, adapt their strategies, and keep moving forward despite temporary setbacks.

- **Consistent Effort Over Time**: Persistence is characterized by consistent effort over time. It's about showing up day after day, putting in the work, and making incremental progress toward your goals, even when the results may not be immediately visible. This sustained effort gradually builds momentum and propels you closer to success.

- **Adaptability and Flexibility**: While persistence involves staying committed to your goals, it also requires a degree of adaptability and flexibility. Sometimes, unforeseen circumstances may necessitate adjusting your approach or pivoting to a new direction. Being open to change and willing to adapt your strategies can help you overcome obstacles more effectively.

- **Positive Mindset and Self-Belief**: A positive mindset and self-belief are essential components of persistence. Believing in your abilities, maintaining optimism in the face of challenges, and reframing setbacks as opportunities for growth can bolster your resilience and keep you motivated to persevere.

- **Focus on the Process**: Rather than being solely outcome-focused, persistence involves embracing the process of growth and development. It's about enjoying the journey, appreciating small victories, and staying committed to continual improvement. By focusing on the process, you can maintain motivation and sustain your efforts over the long term.

- **Seeking Support and Resources**: Persistence doesn't mean you have to go it alone. Seeking support from mentors, peers, or professionals can provide encouragement, guidance, and resources to help you overcome challenges and stay on track toward your goals. Surrounding yourself with a supportive network can bolster your resilience and motivation.

- **Celebrating Progress**: Recognize and celebrate your progress along the way. Acknowledge your achievements, no matter how small, and use them as fuel to keep pushing forward. Celebrating milestones reinforces your sense of accomplishment and provides encouragement to continue persisting toward your goals.

- **Learning and Growth Mindset**: Adopt a learning and growth mindset, recognizing that setbacks and failures are opportunities for learning and personal growth. Embrace challenges as chances to develop new skills, gain valuable insights, and become stronger and more resilient along the way.

- **Perseverance Despite Doubt**: Finally, persistence often involves pushing forward even when doubt creeps in. It's normal to experience moments of uncertainty or self-doubt, but persistent individuals choose to push through these feelings and keep acting toward their goals, trusting in their abilities and the process.

CHAPTER 2

The Psychology of Persistence

What drives some individuals to persist in the face of seemingly insurmountable challenges, while others falter and retreat? In this chapter, we delve into the psychology of persistence, exploring the cognitive and emotional factors that influence our ability to persevere. We discuss concepts such as grit, resilience, and determination, and examine how beliefs, mindset, and self-talk shape our willingness to persist in the pursuit of our goals.

The psychology of persistence delves into the underlying cognitive, emotional, and behavioral processes that drive individuals to persevere in the pursuit of their goals despite obstacles and setbacks. Here are some key psychological factors that contribute to persistence:

- **Goal Setting and Motivation:** Persistence often begins with setting clear, achievable goals that are personally meaningful and motivating. Goals provide a sense of direction and purpose, serving as powerful drivers of behavior. When individuals have a strong desire to achieve their goals, they are more likely to persist in the face of challenges.

- **Self-Efficacy:** Self-efficacy refers to an individual's belief in their ability to successfully accomplish tasks and overcome challenges. High self-efficacy is associated with greater persistence, as individuals who believe in their own capabilities are more likely to exert effort and persevere in the face of adversity. Self-efficacy can be cultivated through mastery experiences, social modeling, verbal persuasion, and physiological states.

- **Resilience and Coping Strategies:** Resilience is the ability to bounce back from setbacks and adversity. Persistent individuals are often resilient, employing effective coping strategies to manage stress, regulate emotions, and maintain a positive outlook in the face of challenges. These coping strategies may include problem-solving, seeking social support, reframing negative thoughts, and practicing self-care.

- **Optimism and Positive Thinking:** Optimism involves maintaining a positive outlook and expecting favorable outcomes, even in the face of difficulties. Optimistic individuals are more likely to persevere through setbacks, viewing obstacles as temporary and surmountable rather than insurmountable barriers. Cultivating optimism and practicing positive thinking can bolster persistence and resilience.

- **Intrinsic and Extrinsic Motivation:** Motivation plays a crucial role in persistence, whether it stems from intrinsic factors (such as personal interest, enjoyment, or satisfaction) or extrinsic factors (such as rewards, recognition, or external pressure). While extrinsic motivators can provide initial impetus, intrinsic motivation is often more sustainable and enduring, driving individuals to persist in the absence of external rewards.

- **Mindset and Attributional Style:** Mindset refers to individuals' beliefs about the nature of abilities and intelligence. A growth mindset, characterized by the belief that abilities can be developed through effort and learning, fosters persistence and resilience. Conversely, a fixed mindset, which views abilities as fixed traits, may hinder persistence by leading individuals to avoid challenges and give up easily. Attributional style, or how individuals attribute success and failure, also influences persistence. Those who attribute failure to external factors that are controllable and changeable are more likely to persist in the face of adversity.

- **Self-Regulation and Willpower:** Persistence often requires self-regulation—the ability to control impulses, manage distractions, and stay focused on long-term goals. Willpower, or self-control, is a key component of self-regulation and plays a vital role in overcoming procrastination, resisting temptation, and persevering through challenging tasks. Strengthening self-regulatory skills can enhance persistence and goal attainment.

- **Feedback and Reinforcement:** Feedback and reinforcement play a crucial role in shaping persistence. Positive feedback and reinforcement for progress and effort can increase motivation and encourage continued persistence. Constructive feedback that provides guidance and support for improvement can also bolster persistence by helping individuals learn from setbacks and adjust their strategies accordingly.

Understanding the psychological factors that underlie persistence can empower individuals to cultivate this essential quality and harness it to overcome obstacles, achieve their goals, and ultimately lead more fulfilling lives. By leveraging strategies to enhance motivation, resilience, self-efficacy, and self-regulation, individuals can develop the mindset and skills needed to persist in the pursuit of their aspirations.

CHAPTER 3

Overcoming Obstacles with Persistence

Obstacles are inevitable on the path to success, but with persistence, they can become steppingstones rather than stumbling blocks. In this chapter, we explore strategies for overcoming obstacles with persistence. We discuss the importance of resilience, flexibility, and problem-solving skills in navigating challenges effectively. Through case studies and practical examples, we demonstrate how persistence can turn setbacks into opportunities for growth and advancement.

Overcoming obstacles with persistence involves adopting a resilient mindset and employing effective strategies to navigate challenges and setbacks. Here's how you can leverage persistence to overcome obstacles:

- **Maintain a Positive Mindset:** Cultivate optimism and maintain a positive outlook, even in the face of adversity. Believe in your ability to overcome challenges and trust that setbacks are temporary setbacks, not permanent barriers.

- **Set Clear Goals:** Define your goals with clarity and specificity, breaking them down into manageable steps. Clear goals provide direction and motivation, helping you stay focused and determined in the face of obstacles.

- **Stay Flexible and Adapt**: Be open to adjusting your approach and strategies when faced with obstacles. If one method doesn't work, try another. Embrace change and be willing to pivot when necessary to find alternative solutions.

- **Seek Support**: Don't hesitate to reach out for support from friends, family, mentors, or colleagues when facing obstacles. Surround yourself with a supportive network of individuals who can offer encouragement, advice, and assistance.

- **Practice Resilience**: Develop resilience by viewing obstacles as opportunities for growth and learning. Reframe setbacks as valuable experiences that can strengthen your skills, knowledge, and character. Focus on what you can control and take proactive steps to move forward.

- **Break Tasks into Smaller Steps**: When faced with a daunting obstacle, break it down into smaller, more manageable tasks. By tackling one step at a time, you can make progress and build momentum toward overcoming the larger obstacle.

- **Persist Through Perseverance**: Stay committed to your goals and persist in your efforts, even when progress seems slow, or obstacles appear insurmountable. Remember that persistence often leads to breakthroughs, and every step forward brings you closer to success.

- **Learn from Setbacks**: Embrace setbacks as opportunities for reflection and learning. Analyze what went wrong, identify lessons learned, and use this knowledge to refine your approach and make improvements for future endeavors.

- **Focus on Solutions**: Instead of dwelling on problems, focus your energy on finding solutions. Adopt a solution-oriented mindset and brainstorm creative ways to overcome obstacles. Take proactive steps to address challenges and move toward your goals.

- **Celebrate Progress**: Acknowledge and celebrate your progress, no matter how small. Recognize your achievements and use them as motivation to keep pushing forward. Celebrating milestones along the way boosts morale and reinforces your commitment to overcoming obstacles with persistence.

By adopting a positive mindset, setting clear goals, seeking support, practicing resilience, and persisting through challenges, you can overcome obstacles with persistence and ultimately achieve your goals. Remember that setbacks are a natural part of the journey, and each obstacle you overcome brings you one step closer to success.

CHAPTER 4

Learning from Failure and Setbacks

Failure is an inevitable part of the journey toward success, but it is how we respond to failure that determines our ultimate outcome. In this chapter, we explore the role of failure and setbacks in the process of persistence. We discuss the importance of reframing failure as a learning opportunity, embracing resilience, and maintaining a growth mindset in the face of adversity. We illustrate the transformative power of persistence in overcoming setbacks and achieving success.

Learning from failure and setbacks is essential for personal growth, resilience, and ultimately, success. Here's how you can effectively learn from failure and setbacks:

- **Acceptance and Reflection:** Instead of denying or ignoring failure, accept it as a natural part of the learning process. Take the time to reflect on what went wrong and why. Consider factors within your control as well as external circumstances that may have contributed to the setback.

- **Identify Lessons Learned**: Look for lessons and insights that can be gleaned from the experience. What did you learn about yourself, your approach, or the situation? Identify specific actions or decisions that contributed to the setback and consider how you can approach similar situations differently in the future.

- **Adjust and Adapt:** Use the lessons learned to adjust your strategies, behaviors, or mindset moving forward. Consider what changes you can make to improve your approach or mitigate potential risks in the future. Embrace flexibility and adaptability as you incorporate these learnings into your ongoing efforts.

- **Focus on Growth, Not Failure:** Shift your perspective from viewing failure as a measure of your worth or abilities to seeing it as an opportunity for growth and improvement. Embrace a growth mindset, which recognizes that abilities can be developed through effort and learning. See setbacks as temporary setbacks rather than permanent failures.

- **Seek Feedback and Perspective:** Reach out to trusted mentors, colleagues, or friends for feedback and perspective on the situation. Their insights can offer valuable perspectives and help you gain clarity on areas for improvement. Be open to constructive criticism and use it as a catalyst for growth.

- **Practice Self-Compassion:** Be kind and compassionate toward yourself during times of failure or setback. Acknowledge the disappointment or frustration you may feel, but avoid dwelling on self-criticism or negative self-talk. Treat yourself with the same kindness and understanding you would offer to a friend facing a similar situation.

- **Persist with Resilience**: Use failure as motivation to persevere and continue pursuing your goals with resilience and determination. Recognize that setbacks are inevitable on the path to success and that each failure brings you one step closer to achieving your objectives. Embrace challenges as opportunities to learn, grow, and ultimately succeed.

- **Celebrate Progress and Successes**: Take time to celebrate your progress and successes, no matter how small. Acknowledge your efforts and achievements along the way and use them as reminders of your resilience and ability to overcome obstacles. Celebrating milestones boosts morale and reinforces your commitment to learning and growth.

By approaching failure and setbacks with a constructive mindset, embracing the lessons learned, and persisting with resilience and determination, you can turn setbacks into opportunities for personal and professional development. Remember that failure is not the end of the road but rather a steppingstone on the journey to success.

CHAPTER 5

The Role of Persistence in Goal Achievement

Goals provide the roadmap for our journey, but it is persistence that propels us forward and keeps us on course. In this chapter, we explore the symbiotic relationship between persistence and goal achievement. We discuss strategies for setting SMART goals, breaking them down into manageable steps, and maintaining momentum through consistent action and perseverance. Through practical tips and insights, we empower readers to harness the power of persistence to achieve their most ambitious goals and aspirations.

Persistence plays a crucial role in goal achievement by providing the necessary drive, resilience, and determination to overcome obstacles and setbacks encountered along the way. Here's how persistence contributes to the attainment of goals:

- **Maintaining Motivation:** Setting and pursuing meaningful goals requires sustained motivation over time. Persistence helps individuals stay motivated even when faced with challenges, setbacks, or delays. It fuels the determination to keep moving forward despite obstacles, keeping the goal in sight and maintaining momentum.

▪ **Overcoming Obstacles:** Pursuing goals inevitably involves encountering obstacles, setbacks, and failures. Persistence enables individuals to navigate these challenges with resilience and determination. Rather than giving up at the first sign of difficulty, persistent individuals view obstacles as opportunities for growth and learning. They persistently seek solutions, adapt their strategies, and persevere until they find a way forward.

▪ **Fostering Resilience:** Resilience is the ability to bounce back from setbacks and adversity. Persistent individuals develop resilience by facing and overcoming obstacles along the path to their goals. Each setback they encounter strengthens their resolve and reinforces their belief in their ability to overcome challenges. This resilience enables them to persevere through difficult times and stay focused on their objectives.

▪ **Building Momentum:** Persistence builds momentum over time as individuals make consistent progress toward their goals. Each small step forward contributes to a sense of accomplishment and reinforces the commitment to continue moving forward. As momentum builds, progress accelerates, and individuals gain confidence in their ability to achieve their goals.

- **Developing Discipline and Self-Control:** Persistence requires discipline and self-control to stay focused on long-term goals despite short-term distractions or temptations. It involves making sacrifices, prioritizing tasks, and staying committed to the actions necessary for goal attainment. Through consistent effort and self-discipline, persistent individuals make steady progress toward their objectives.

- **Achieving Mastery:** Mastery of skills or knowledge often requires prolonged effort and practice. Persistence enables individuals to persevere through the challenges and setbacks inherent in the learning process. Whether mastering a musical instrument, learning a new language, or developing expertise in a profession, persistent individuals are willing to invest the time and effort required to achieve mastery.

- **Cultivating Confidence and Self-Efficacy:** Success breeds confidence, and persistence contributes to the development of confidence and self-efficacy—the belief in one's ability to succeed. Each accomplishment along the way reinforces individuals' belief in their capabilities and strengthens their confidence in their ability to achieve their goals. This self-belief fuels further persistence and enhances the likelihood of success.

- **Realizing Long-Term Vision**: Many goals require sustained effort over an extended period to achieve. Persistence enables individuals to maintain focus on their long-term vision, even when immediate results may not be forthcoming. By staying committed to their objectives and persistently pursuing them over time, individuals can ultimately realize their aspirations and bring their long-term vision to fruition.

In summary, persistence is a critical factor in goal achievement, providing the determination, resilience, and discipline needed to overcome obstacles, maintain motivation, and realize long-term objectives. By cultivating a persistent mindset and consistently applying effort toward their goals, individuals can increase their likelihood of success and achieve meaningful outcomes in their personal and professional lives.

CHAPTER 6

Nurturing Persistence in Relationships

Persistence is not limited to individual pursuits—it is also essential for nurturing meaningful relationships and connections. In this chapter, we explore how persistence manifests in the context of relationships. We discuss the importance of communication, empathy, and commitment in building strong, enduring bonds with others. Additionally, we examine strategies for navigating conflicts and challenges with resilience and determination, fostering trust, understanding, and mutual support in relationships.

Nurturing persistence in relationships involves fostering resilience, commitment, and perseverance to overcome challenges and maintain strong connections over time. Here are some ways to cultivate persistence in relationships:

- **Commitment to Growth:** Approach relationships with a commitment to growth and personal development. Recognize that challenges and conflicts are natural aspects of any relationship and view them as opportunities for learning and strengthening the connection.

- **Effective Communication:** Communicate openly, honestly, and respectfully with your partner or loved ones. Share your thoughts, feelings, and concerns openly, and be willing to listen attentively to their perspective. Effective communication fosters understanding, empathy, and connection, laying the foundation for persistence in the relationship.

- **Resilience in Adversity**: Cultivate resilience to navigate through difficult times and overcome setbacks together. When faced with challenges, approach them as a team, supporting each other and working collaboratively to find solutions. Trust in your ability to weather storms together and emerge stronger from adversity.

- **Shared Goals and Values**: Identify shared goals, values, and aspirations that unite you and your partner or loved ones. Having a common vision for the future can provide a sense of purpose and direction, motivating you to persist through challenges in pursuit of your shared goals.

- **Empathy and Understanding:** Practice empathy and understanding in your interactions with others. Seek to understand their perspective, feelings, and needs, even when you may disagree or face conflicts. Empathy strengthens emotional bonds and fosters a sense through challenges together.

- **Celebrate Achievements of connection, making it easier to persist** : Acknowledge and celebrate milestones and achievements in your relationship, no matter how small. Celebrating successes together reinforces the bond between you and your partner or loved ones and encourages continued persistence in working towards shared goals.

- **Adaptability and Flexibility:** Be willing to adapt and adjust to changing circumstances in your relationship. Life is dynamic, and being flexible in your approach allows you to navigate transitions and challenges more effectively. Embrace change as an opportunity for growth and evolution in your relationship.

- **Forgiveness and Letting Go:** Practice forgiveness and let go of past grievances or resentments that may hinder the progress of your relationship. Holding onto grudges only serves to create barriers to connection and persistence. Instead, focus on resolving conflicts constructively and moving forward with a renewed sense of commitment and understanding.

- **Quality Time Together:** Make time for quality moments together, whether it's through shared activities, meaningful conversations, or simply enjoying each other's company. Prioritize nurturing your connection and fostering intimacy, as these moments of connection strengthen your bond and encourage persistence in the relationship.

- **Support and Encouragement:** Offer support and encouragement to your partner or loved ones during challenging times. Be their cheerleader, offering reassurance, guidance, and assistance as needed. Knowing that you have each other's backs can provide the motivation and resilience needed to persist through obstacles together.

By nurturing persistence in your relationships through effective communication, resilience, shared goals, empathy, adaptability, and support, you can cultivate strong, enduring connections that thrive in the face of challenges and adversity.

CHAPTER 7

The Ripple Effect of Persistence

The impact of persistence extends far beyond individual achievement—it creates a ripple effect that inspires and empowers others to strive for greatness. In this chapter, we explore how acts of persistence can inspire change and transformation on a broader scale. We discuss the power of leading by example, sharing stories of perseverance and triumph that ignite hope and motivation in others. Through collective action and solidarity, we can harness the ripple effect of persistence to create a better, more resilient world for future generations.

- **Personal Growth and Development:** When individuals persistently pursue their goals, they experience personal growth and development. Overcoming challenges, learning from setbacks, and achieving success contribute to increased confidence, resilience, and self-efficacy. This personal growth creates a ripple effect, positively impacting other areas of their lives and relationships.

- **Inspiration and Motivation:** The persistent efforts of individuals can inspire and motivate others to pursue their own goals and aspirations. Witnessing someone overcome obstacles and achieve success through perseverance can serve as a powerful example, inspiring others to act and strive for their dreams.

- **Positive Impact on Relationships**: Persistent individuals often bring determination, resilience, and commitment into their relationships. Their ability to navigate challenges, communicate effectively, and work towards shared goals can positively influence their partners, family members, and friends. This ripple effect fosters stronger, more resilient relationships built on trust and mutual support.

- **Innovation and Progress**: Persistence drives innovation and progress by fueling the relentless pursuit of solutions to complex problems. Individuals who persistently pursue creative ideas, research, and inventions contribute to advancements in science, technology, business, and society. These innovations have a ripple effect, benefiting countless individuals and shaping the world we live in.

- **Community and Social Change**: Persistent individuals often play a crucial role in driving positive change within their communities and society. Whether advocating for social justice, environmental sustainability, or humanitarian causes, their determination to create meaningful impact inspires others to join their efforts. This collective action creates a ripple effect, leading to tangible changes and improvements in the world.

- **Resilience in the Face of Adversity:** The ripple effect of persistence is particularly evident during times of adversity and crisis. Individuals who persistently strive to overcome challenges, support those in need, and rebuild communities in the aftermath of disasters demonstrate the power of resilience and solidarity. Their actions inspire hope, foster resilience, and create a ripple effect of compassion and unity.

- **Legacy and Long-Term Impact:** The ripple effect of persistence extends beyond the present moment and influences future generations. Individuals who persistently work towards their goals leave a legacy of determination, resilience, and achievement that inspires others long after they are gone. Their actions shape the trajectory of future generations, leaving a lasting impact on society.

- **Cultural and Societal Shifts:** Persistent efforts to challenge norms, break down barriers, and promote inclusivity can lead to cultural and societal shifts. Individuals who persistently advocate for equality, diversity, and social justice contribute to creating a more inclusive and equitable society. Their actions have a ripple effect, catalyzing positive change and shaping collective attitudes and behaviors.

In essence, the ripple effect of persistence is a powerful force that creates positive change at individual, interpersonal, community, and societal levels. By embracing determination, resilience, and commitment in pursuit of their goals, individuals can inspire others, drive innovation, foster stronger relationships, and contribute to a more resilient and compassionate world.

CHAPTER 8

Embracing Persistence as a Way of Life

In this chapter, we reflect on the profound significance of persistence in shaping our destinies and transforming our lives. We emphasize the importance of embracing persistence as a way of life—a guiding principle that empowers us to overcome obstacles, achieve our goals, and realize our fullest potential. By cultivating resilience, determination, and unwavering faith in our abilities, we can navigate life's challenges with courage, grace, and resilience, knowing that with persistence as our ally, anything is possible. Let us embark on this journey of self-discovery and growth, knowing that with persistence as our compass, we can chart a course toward a future filled with limitless possibilities and boundless potential.

Embracing persistence as a way of life involves adopting a mindset and lifestyle characterized by determination, resilience, and commitment to ongoing growth and achievement. Here's how you can embrace persistence as a way of life:

- **Set Clear Goals and Vision:** Define your long-term goals and vision for your life, career, relationships, and personal development. Clarify what you want to achieve and why it's meaningful to you. Having a clear sense of purpose and direction provides motivation and guides your persistent efforts.

- **Develop a Growth Mindset:** Cultivate a growth mindset, which focuses on learning, improvement, and resilience. Embrace challenges as opportunities for growth, view failures as learning experiences, and believe in your ability to develop skills and overcome obstacles through effort and perseverance.

- **Take Consistent Action:** Take consistent, purposeful action towards your goals every day, regardless of how small or incremental it may seem. Commit to making progress, even when faced with setbacks or distractions. Persistence is about showing up consistently and staying focused on your objectives.

- **Embrace Challenges and Setbacks:** Approach challenges and setbacks with resilience and determination. Rather than avoiding difficulties or giving up at the first sign of resistance, see them as opportunities for growth and learning. Persistently seek solutions, adapt your approach, and keep moving forward despite obstacles.

- **Stay Flexible and Adapt:** Be willing to adapt and adjust your plans in response to changing circumstances or new information. Flexibility allows you to navigate uncertainty and setbacks more effectively, finding alternative paths forward when necessary while remaining committed to your overarching goals.

- **Seek Support and Accountability**: Surround yourself with a supportive network of friends, family, mentors, or peers who encourage and motivate you to persist in pursuit of your goals. Share your aspirations and progress with others, and seek their support and accountability to stay on track.

- **Practice Self-Compassion**: Be kind and compassionate towards yourself as you pursue your goals. Acknowledge that setbacks and challenges are a natural part of the journey and treat yourself with understanding and patience. Practice self-care and prioritize your well-being as you persistently pursue your aspirations.

- **Maintain Focus and Discipline**: Stay focused on your priorities and maintain discipline in your actions and habits. Minimize distractions, prioritize tasks, and allocate your time and energy effectively to make progress towards your goals. Persistence requires consistent effort and commitment to staying the course.

- **Embrace a Purpose-Driven Life**: Ultimately, embracing persistence as a way of life is about living with purpose and intentionality. Align your actions with your values and aspirations, and let persistence guide you in pursuing a life that is meaningful, fulfilling, and aligned with your deepest desires.

By adopting a persistent mindset and integrating these principles into your daily life, you can embrace persistence as a way of life and unlock your full potential for growth, achievement, and fulfillment.

CHAPTER 9

The Science of Persistence

B ehind the concept of persistence lies a wealth of scientific research that sheds light on why some individuals exhibit unwavering determination while others falter in the face of adversity. In this chapter, we delve into the science of persistence, exploring the neurological, psychological, and sociological factors that contribute to our ability to persevere. We examine studies on motivation, willpower, and self-regulation, uncovering the underlying mechanisms that drive persistent behavior. By understanding the science behind persistence, we gain valuable insights into how we can cultivate and harness this essential quality to achieve our goals and aspirations.

The science of persistence draws from various fields such as psychology, neuroscience, and behavioral economics to understand the underlying mechanisms and factors that contribute to individuals' ability to persist in pursuing their goals. Here are some key insights from scientific research on persistence:

- **Self-Determination Theory**: Self-Determination Theory (SDT) emphasizes the importance of intrinsic motivation, autonomy, and relatedness in fostering persistence. According to SDT, individuals are more likely to persist in pursuing goals that are aligned with their values, interests, and sense of autonomy. Cultivating intrinsic motivation and creating environments that support autonomy and relatedness can enhance persistence.

- **Grit and Resilience:** Psychologist Angela Duckworth's research on grit has shed light on the importance of perseverance and passion for long-term goals. Gritty individuals demonstrate a combination of passion and perseverance in the pursuit of their goals, even in the face of obstacles and setbacks. Building grit and resilience through deliberate practice, effortful learning, and resilience-building exercises can enhance persistence.

- **Goal Setting and Implementation Intentions**: Goal-setting theory emphasizes the importance of setting specific, challenging, and achievable goals for fostering persistence. Implementation intentions, or specific plans detailing when, where, and how individuals will take action towards their goals, have been shown to enhance goal pursuit and persistence. Breaking goals down into manageable steps and creating implementation intentions can increase the likelihood of persistence.

- **Cognitive Control and Willpower:** Research in cognitive psychology has examined the role of cognitive control and willpower in maintaining focus and resisting temptation while pursuing long-term goals. Strategies such as attentional control, inhibitory control, and cognitive reappraisal can help individuals manage distractions, regulate impulses, and maintain persistence in the face of temptation.

- **Social Support and Accountability:** Social psychology research highlights the importance of social support and accountability in fostering persistence. Having a supportive network of friends, family, or peers who encourage and motivate individuals to pursue their goals can increase persistence. Accountability mechanisms, such as goal-sharing, progress-tracking, and mutual encouragement, can also enhance persistence by fostering a sense of responsibility and commitment.

- **Mindset and Beliefs:** Psychologist Carol Dweck's work on mindset has shown how beliefs about intelligence and abilities influence persistence. Individuals with a growth mindset, who believe that abilities can be developed through effort and learning, are more likely to persist in the face of challenges. Cultivating a growth mindset and reframing setbacks as opportunities for growth can enhance persistence.

- **Behavioral Economics and Nudge Theory:** Behavioral economics research has explored the role of behavioral nudges in influencing persistence and goal pursuit. Nudges, or small changes in the environment that make desired behaviors more likely, can help individuals overcome barriers and maintain persistence. Designing environments that make desired behaviors easy, attractive, and socially normative can enhance persistence.

By integrating insights from the science of persistence into personal goal-setting and behavior change strategies, individuals can cultivate the motivation, resilience, and determination needed to persistently pursue their goals and achieve long-term success.

CHAPTER 10

Building Resilience through Persistence

Resilience is the ability to bounce back from adversity, and persistence is the fuel that powers our resilience. In this chapter, we explore how persistence contributes to building resilience—the capacity to withstand and overcome life's challenges with grace and fortitude. We discuss strategies for cultivating resilience through persistent effort, such as reframing setbacks as opportunities for growth, building a strong support network, and practicing self-care and mindfulness. By embracing persistence as a tool for building resilience, we can navigate life's ups and downs with greater ease and emerge stronger and more resilient in the face of adversity.

Building resilience through persistence involves cultivating the mental and emotional strength to bounce back from setbacks, overcome obstacles, and thrive in the face of adversity. Here's how persistence can help in building resilience:

- **Developing Coping Skills:** Persistence involves facing challenges head-on and persevering through difficulties. As individuals persist in pursuing their goals, they develop and refine coping skills to manage stress, regulate emotions, and cope effectively with setbacks. Over time, these coping skills contribute to greater resilience in the face of adversity.

- **Learning from Setbacks:** Persistent individuals view setbacks as opportunities for growth and learning rather than insurmountable obstacles. By persisting through challenges, they gain valuable insights into their strengths, weaknesses, and areas for improvement. Learning from setbacks enhances resilience by equipping individuals with the knowledge and experience to navigate future challenges more effectively.

- **Building Confidence and Self-Efficacy:** Persistence builds confidence and self-efficacy—the belief in one's ability to overcome challenges and succeed. As individuals persist in pursuing their goals, they accumulate evidence of their competence and capabilities, reinforcing their confidence in their ability to handle adversity. This increased confidence and self-efficacy contribute to greater resilience in the face of future challenges.

- **Promoting Positive Adaptation:** Persistence encourages individuals to adapt and adjust their strategies in response to changing circumstances or setbacks. By persistently seeking solutions and alternative paths forward, individuals develop the flexibility and adaptability needed to navigate uncertainty and adversity. This ability to adapt promotes positive adaptation and resilience in the face of challenges.

- **Fostering Social Support**: Persistent individuals are more likely to seek and receive social support from friends, family, or peers during challenging times. By reaching out for support and connection, they build strong social networks that provide emotional support, encouragement, and practical assistance. Social support enhances resilience by buffering against the negative effects of stress and adversity.

- **Maintaining Focus on Goals and Values**: Persistence involves staying focused on long-term goals and values, even in the face of obstacles or setbacks. By maintaining a sense of purpose and direction, individuals are better able to navigate adversity and stay motivated during difficult times. This clarity of purpose promotes resilience by providing a source of meaning and motivation.

- **Cultivating Optimism and Positive Thinking**: Persistent individuals tend to maintain an optimistic outlook and positive attitude, even in the face of adversity. By reframing setbacks as temporary and surmountable challenges, they maintain hope and confidence in their ability to overcome obstacles.

This optimism and positive thinking contribute to greater resilience by fostering a resilient mindset and promoting adaptive coping strategies.

By persisting through challenges, learning from setbacks, and cultivating resilience-building skills and attitudes, individuals can enhance their ability to bounce back from adversity, thrive in the face of challenges, and lead more fulfilling lives.

CHAPTER 11

The Role of Persistence in Mental Health

Mental health is intricately linked to our ability to persist in the face of challenges and setbacks. In this chapter, we explore the role of persistence in promoting mental health and well-being. We discuss how persistent effort can help build self-esteem, foster a sense of purpose and meaning, and enhance overall psychological resilience. Additionally, we examine how practices such as mindfulness, gratitude, and self-compassion can complement persistence in promoting mental and emotional well-being. By prioritizing persistence and self-care, we can cultivate a resilient mindset that empowers us to navigate life's challenges with greater ease and grace.

Persistence plays a significant role in mental health by contributing to resilience, coping abilities, and overall well-being. Here's how persistence impacts mental health:

- **Resilience Building:** Persistence fosters resilience—the ability to bounce back from adversity, trauma, or stress. Individuals who persistently face and overcome challenges develop resilience over time. They learn to adapt to difficult situations, cope effectively with stressors, and maintain a sense of balance and well-being even in the face of adversity.

▪ **Coping with Stress:** Persistent individuals tend to have stronger coping skills, enabling them to manage stress more effectively. They approach challenges with a problem-solving mindset, seek support when needed, and utilize healthy coping strategies such as exercise, mindfulness, and relaxation techniques. These coping mechanisms help mitigate the negative effects of stress on mental health and promote overall well-being.

▪ **Enhanced Self-Efficacy:** Persistence contributes to greater self-efficacy—the belief in one's ability to accomplish tasks and overcome challenges. Individuals who persistently pursue their goals and overcome obstacles develop a sense of competence and mastery. This increased self-efficacy boosts confidence, reduces feelings of helplessness, and promotes a positive outlook on life, all of which are beneficial for mental health.

▪ **Reduced Risk of Depression and Anxiety:** Persistent individuals are less likely to experience depression and anxiety because they are better equipped to cope with stressors and setbacks. By persistently pursuing their goals and maintaining a sense of purpose and direction, they are less susceptible to feelings of hopelessness, helplessness, and rumination, which are common risk factors for depression and anxiety.

- **Promotion of Growth Mindset:** Persistence is closely linked to a growth mindset—the belief that abilities can be developed through effort and learning. Individuals with a growth mindset are more resilient in the face of challenges and setbacks. They view failures as opportunities for growth and learning, rather than as reflections of their inherent worth or abilities. This mindset promotes adaptive coping strategies, resilience, and mental well-being.

- **Sense of Accomplishment and Purpose:** Persistently working towards meaningful goals provides individuals with a sense of accomplishment and purpose, which are essential for mental health and well-being. Achieving goals, overcoming obstacles, and making progress towards desired outcomes contribute to feelings of satisfaction, fulfillment, and happiness.

- **Improved Self-Regulation:** Persistence involves self-regulation—the ability to control impulses, manage emotions, and stay focused on long-term goals. Individuals who persistently pursue their goals develop stronger self-regulation skills, which are essential for mental health. They are better able to regulate their emotions, resist temptation, and maintain a sense of balance and well-being.

- **Promotion of Positive Relationships:** Persistent individuals tend to cultivate strong social support networks, which are crucial for mental health and well-being. By persistently investing in relationships, seeking support when needed, and maintaining connections with others, they foster a sense of belonging, connection, and emotional support, which buffer against the negative effects of stress and promote mental well-being.

Overall, persistence plays a vital role in mental health by fostering resilience, coping abilities, self-efficacy, and a positive outlook on life. By persistently pursuing their goals, overcoming challenges, and maintaining a sense of purpose and direction, individuals can enhance their mental health and overall well-being.

CHAPTER 12

Overcoming Procrastination with Persistence

Procrastination is the enemy of progress, but with persistence, it can be overcome. In this chapter, we explore how persistent effort can help break the cycle of procrastination and boost productivity. We discuss strategies for overcoming procrastination, such as breaking tasks into smaller, more manageable steps, setting deadlines and accountability measures, and practicing self-compassion and forgiveness. By harnessing the power of persistence, we can overcome procrastination and unleash our full potential to achieve our goals and aspirations.

Overcoming procrastination with persistence involves developing strategies and habits that help individuals take consistent action towards their goals, despite the temptation to delay or avoid tasks. Here are some ways to use persistence to overcome procrastination:

- **Set Clear and Specific Goals**: Define your goals with clarity and specificity, breaking them down into manageable tasks. Clear goals provide direction and motivation, making it easier to prioritize tasks and act.

- **Create a Plan of Action:** Develop a detailed plan outlining the steps you need to take to achieve your goals. Break down tasks into smaller, actionable steps and schedule specific times to work on them. Having a clear plan in place makes it easier to overcome the inertia of procrastination and take the first step.

- **Start Small and Build Momentum:** Begin with small, manageable tasks to build momentum and overcome the initial resistance to getting started. Starting small reduces the perceived effort and makes it easier to overcome the inertia of procrastination. Once you get started, you're more likely to continue working on the task.

- **Use the Two-Minute Rule:** Apply the two-minute rule, which involves committing to working on a task for just two minutes. Often, getting started is the hardest part, and once you overcome the initial resistance, you'll find it easier to continue working on the task.

- **Practice Self-Compassion:** Be kind and understanding towards yourself when you struggle with procrastination. Avoid self-criticism and negative self-talk, which can further fuel procrastination. Instead, practice self-compassion and remind yourself that it's okay to make mistakes or struggle with motivation from time to time.

- **Visualize Success**: Visualize yourself completing the task and achieving your goals. Imagine how it will feel to accomplish what you set out to do and use that positive vision as motivation to overcome procrastination and act.

- **Set Deadlines and Accountability**: Set deadlines for yourself to create a sense of urgency and accountability. Break down larger goals into smaller, time-bound milestones and hold yourself accountable for meeting them. You can also enlist the support of a friend, family member, or colleague to hold you accountable and provide encouragement.

- **Use Rewards and Incentives**: Reward yourself for making progress or achieving milestones along the way. Use incentives such as breaks, treats, or enjoyable activities to motivate yourself to act and overcome procrastination.

- **Identify and Address Procrastination Triggers**: Pay attention to the specific situations, emotions, or thoughts that trigger procrastination for you. Once you identify your triggers, develop strategies to address them effectively. This may involve setting boundaries, managing distractions, or addressing underlying fears or anxieties.

- **Practice Persistence and Consistency**: Above all, cultivate a persistent mindset and commit to taking consistent action towards your goals, even when faced with resistance or setbacks. Persistence is key to overcoming procrastination and achieving long-term success.

By combining persistence with these strategies, you can overcome procrastination and make meaningful progress towards your goals, one step at a time. Remember that overcoming procrastination is a skill that can be developed with practice and consistency.

CHAPTER 13

Cultivating Persistence in Children and Adolescents

Persistence is a skill that can be cultivated from a young age, setting the stage for lifelong success and fulfillment. In this chapter, we explore strategies for nurturing persistence in children and adolescents. We discuss the importance of fostering a growth mindset, praising effort over innate ability, and providing opportunities for challenge and mastery. Additionally, we examine how parental modeling and support can influence children's persistence and resilience. By instilling the value of persistence early on, we can empower the next generation to navigate life's challenges with confidence, resilience, and determination.

Cultivating persistence in children and adolescents is crucial for their personal development, academic success, and overall well-being. Here are some strategies parents, educators, and caregivers can use to foster persistence in young people:

- **Set Clear Expectations:** Clearly communicate expectations regarding effort, perseverance, and resilience. Encourage children to take on challenges and embrace the learning process, emphasizing that mistakes and setbacks are natural parts of learning and growth.

- **Model Persistence:** Serve as a role model by demonstrating persistence in your own pursuits and endeavors. Children learn by observing the behaviors of adults around them, so modeling persistence in the face of challenges sets a powerful example for them to follow.

- **Provide Supportive Feedback:** Offer constructive feedback that focuses on effort, progress, and strategies rather than just outcomes. Praise children for their hard work, resilience, and perseverance, reinforcing the importance of persistence in achieving goals.

- **Encourage Goal Setting:** Help children set specific, achievable goals that align with their interests and aspirations. Break down larger goals into smaller, manageable tasks, and encourage children to create action plans for achieving them. Goal setting provides a sense of direction and motivation, fostering persistence in pursuit of objectives.

- **Promote a Growth Mindset:** Cultivate a growth mindset—the belief that abilities can be developed through effort and practice. Encourage children to view challenges as opportunities for growth and learning, rather than as threats to their abilities. Teach them to embrace mistakes as valuable learning experiences and to persistently seek improvement over time.

- **Provide Opportunities for Mastery:** Offer children opportunities to engage in activities that allow them to develop skills and expertise over time. Whether it's sports, arts, music, or academics, encourage them to pursue activities they enjoy and to persistently practice and improve their abilities.

- **Teach Problem-Solving Skills:** Teach children problem-solving skills and strategies for overcoming obstacles. Help them break down problems into smaller, more manageable components, brainstorm alternative solutions, and consider the potential consequences of their actions. By equipping children with problem-solving skills, you empower them to navigate challenges with confidence and persistence.

- **Foster Resilience:** Help children develop resilience—the ability to bounce back from setbacks and adversity. Encourage them to cope adaptively with stress, regulate their emotions, and seek support from trusted adults when needed. By fostering resilience, you enable children to persist in the face of obstacles and to thrive in challenging situations.

- **Celebrate Effort and Progress**: Celebrate children's efforts, progress, and achievements along the way, no matter how small. Recognize their perseverance, resilience, and determination, and praise their willingness to take on challenges and persist in the face of setbacks. Positive reinforcement reinforces the importance of persistence and encourages children to continue striving towards their goals.

- **Provide a Supportive Environment**: Create a supportive environment that encourages children to take risks, explore their interests, and pursue their passions. Foster a culture of curiosity, creativity, and resilience, where children feel empowered to experiment, make mistakes, and learn from failure without fear of judgment or criticism.

By implementing these strategies consistently and nurturing a supportive environment that values persistence and resilience, parents, educators, and caregivers can help children and adolescents develop the skills and attitudes they need to thrive academically, socially, and personally.

CHAPTER 14

The Ethical Dimension of Persistence

While persistence is often celebrated as a virtue, it is essential to consider its ethical implications. In this chapter, we explore the ethical dimension of persistence, examining when and how persistence can become problematic or harmful. We discuss the importance of ethical reflection and self-awareness in guiding our persistent efforts, ensuring that they align with our values and principles. Additionally, we examine how persistence intersects with concepts such as perseverance, resilience, and moral courage. By approaching persistence with ethical mindfulness, we can harness its power for positive change and contribute to a more just, compassionate, and sustainable world.

The ethical dimension of persistence encompasses the considerations and principles that guide how individuals persist in pursuing their goals while also respecting the rights, well-being, and dignity of others. Here are some key aspects of the ethical dimension of persistence:

- **Ethical persistence:** Ethical Persistence involves respecting the boundaries, autonomy, and well-being of others. It requires individuals to consider the impact of their actions on those around them and to refrain from persisting in ways that infringe upon others' rights or cause harm.

- **Integrity and Honesty**: Ethical persistence entails maintaining integrity and honesty in the pursuit of goals. It requires individuals to uphold ethical standards and principles, even in the face of challenges or temptations to take shortcuts or engage in dishonest behavior.

- **Empathy and Compassion:** Ethical persistence is grounded in empathy and compassion for others. It involves considering the perspectives, needs, and feelings of others and acting with kindness and understanding. Ethical persistence seeks to uplift and support others rather than trample over them in pursuit of individual goals.

- **Fairness and Justice:** Ethical persistence involves striving for fairness and justice in interactions with others. It requires individuals to consider the distribution of benefits and burdens and to ensure that their persistence does not unfairly disadvantage or exploit others.

- **Consent and Boundaries**: Ethical persistence respects the boundaries and consent of others. It involves seeking permission, respecting limits, and honoring the autonomy of individuals in all interactions. Ethical persistence requires individuals to recognize and respect when others indicate a desire to disengage or set boundaries.

- **Responsibility and Accountability**: Ethical persistence entails taking responsibility for one's actions and their consequences. It involves acknowledging mistakes, learning from failures, and making amends when necessary. Ethical persistence also requires individuals to be accountable for the impact of their persistence on others and to take steps to mitigate harm.

- **Sustainability and Long-Term Impact**: Ethical persistence considers the long-term impact of actions on individuals, communities, and the environment. It involves pursuing goals in a way that is sustainable and mindful of the broader consequences. Ethical persistence seeks to create positive, lasting change while minimizing harm and promoting well-being for all.

- **Reflection and Adaptation**: Ethical persistence involves ongoing reflection and adaptation based on feedback and new information. It requires individuals to regularly assess their goals, methods, and impact on others and to adjust their approach as needed to ensure alignment with ethical principles.

- **Balancing Competing Priorities**: Ethical persistence requires individuals to balance their pursuit of goals with other important priorities, such as relationships, health, and well-being. It involves recognizing when persistence may need to be tempered or redirected to prioritize the greater good and the welfare of all involved.

- **Cultural Sensitivity and Diversity**: Ethical persistence acknowledges and respects cultural differences, diversity, and individual differences in values and perspectives. It involves being sensitive to the needs and beliefs of others and avoiding actions that may perpetuate stereotypes or marginalize certain groups.

In summary, the ethical dimension of persistence emphasizes the importance of pursuing goals in a way that respects the rights, well-being, and dignity of others, upholds ethical principles, and contributes to positive outcomes for individuals and society. Ethical persistence involves balancing personal ambition with empathy, integrity, and a commitment to fairness, justice, and sustainability.

CHAPTER 15

Cultivating Persistence in the Face of Adversity

Adversity is a natural part of life, but it is our response to adversity that defines us. In this chapter, we explore how persistence can help us navigate and overcome adversity. We discuss strategies for cultivating persistence in the face of adversity, such as reframing challenges as opportunities for growth, seeking support from others, and maintaining a sense of hope and optimism. Through inspiring stories of individuals who have overcome seemingly insurmountable odds, we illustrate the transformative power of persistence in turning adversity into triumph.

Cultivating persistence in the face of adversity involves developing the mindset, strategies, and habits that enable individuals to persevere and overcome challenges, setbacks, and obstacles. Here are some ways to cultivate persistence in adversity:

- **Maintain a Growth Mindset**: Embrace a growth mindset—the belief that abilities can be developed through effort and practice. View adversity as an opportunity for growth and learning, rather than as a barrier to success. Cultivate a positive outlook and resilience in the face of setbacks.

- **Set Meaningful Goals:** Define clear, meaningful goals that provide direction and purpose. When faced with adversity, remind yourself of the reasons why your goals are important to you. Having a sense of purpose and direction can motivate you to persist through difficult times.

- **Break Down Goals into Manageable Steps**: Break down larger goals into smaller, more manageable steps. Focus on taking one step at a time, rather than feeling overwhelmed by the enormity of the challenge. Celebrate small victories along the way to maintain momentum and motivation.

- **Seek Support and Encouragement:** Reach out to friends, family, mentors, or support groups for encouragement and support during challenging times. Surround yourself with people who believe in you and can provide emotional support, guidance, and encouragement when needed.

- **Practice Self-Compassion:** Be kind and compassionate towards yourself when facing adversity. Avoid self-blame or harsh self-criticism, which can undermine your resilience and persistence. Instead, practice self-compassion by acknowledging your efforts and strengths, and treating yourself with kindness and understanding.

- **Visualize Success**: Visualize yourself overcoming obstacles and achieving your goals, even in the face of adversity. Use visualization techniques to imagine yourself persisting through challenges with confidence and determination. Visualizing success can help reinforce your belief in your ability to overcome adversity.

- **Focus on Solutions, Not Problems**: When faced with adversity, focus on finding solutions rather than dwelling on the problems. Adopt a problem-solving mindset and approach challenges with a proactive attitude. Brainstorm alternative strategies, seek advice from others, and take action to address obstacles head-on.

- **Learn from Setbacks and Failures**: View setbacks and failures as opportunities for growth and learning. Reflect on what went wrong, identify lessons learned, and use that knowledge to adapt your approach and improve future outcomes. Embrace a mindset of continuous improvement and resilience in the face of adversity.

- **Stay Flexible and Adapt**: Be willing to adapt and adjust your strategies in response to changing circumstances or unexpected obstacles. Persistence does not mean sticking to a rigid plan at all costs, but rather being flexible and resourceful in finding alternative paths forward.

- **Stay Committed to Your Values**: Stay true to your core values and principles, even in the face of adversity. Let your values guide your actions and decisions, and draw strength from your sense of integrity and purpose. Remember that persistence is not just about achieving goals, but also about staying true to who you are and what you believe in, even when the going gets tough.

By cultivating persistence in the face of adversity, individuals can develop the resilience, determination, and strength needed to overcome challenges and achieve their goals, even in the most difficult circumstances.

CHAPTER 16

The Legacy of Persistence

The legacy we leave behind is a testament to the persistence and determination with which we pursued our dreams and aspirations. In this chapter, we reflect on the legacy of persistence, exploring how our persistent efforts can inspire and empower others to follow in our footsteps. We discuss the importance of living with purpose and passion, leaving a positive impact on the world, and creating a legacy that endures for generations to come. By embracing persistence as a guiding principle in our lives, we can leave a legacy of resilience, courage, and hope the legacy of persistence is profound and far-reaching, impacting individuals, communities, and societies for generations to come. Here are some aspects of the legacy of persistence:

- **Personal Achievement and Success:** The legacy of persistence is often reflected in the personal achievements and successes of individuals who have persevered in pursuit of their goals. Whether in academia, career, sports, arts, or other endeavors, individuals who persistently overcome obstacles and setbacks leave behind a legacy of accomplishment and excellence.

- **Inspiration and Motivation:** The legacy of persistence inspires and motivates others to pursue their own goals and aspirations. When individuals witness the determination, resilience, and perseverance of those who have achieved success through persistence, they are inspired to overcome their own challenges and strive for greatness.

- **Cultural and Social Change:** Persistence has played a significant role in driving cultural and social change throughout history. Individuals who persistently advocate for justice, equality, and human rights have catalyzed transformative movements and brought about positive change in society. The legacy of their persistence lives on in the progress and advancements they helped to achieve.

- **Innovation and Progress:** The legacy of persistence is evident in the innovations and advancements that have shaped the world. Visionaries, inventors, and entrepreneurs who persistently pursued their ideas and dreams have revolutionized industries, improved lives, and transformed societies. Their legacy of persistence continues to drive innovation and progress in countless fields.

- **Resilience in Adversity:** The legacy of persistence is seen in the resilience and strength of individuals and communities who have faced adversity. Whether overcoming personal hardships, natural disasters, or societal challenges, those who persistently persevere in the face of adversity leave behind a legacy of resilience and courage that inspires others to do the same.

- **Educational and Cultural Legacy:** The legacy of persistence is passed down through generations as part of our educational and cultural heritage. Stories of perseverance and triumph, whether from history, literature, or folklore, serve as sources of inspiration and moral guidance for future generations. They teach valuable lessons about the power of persistence and resilience in overcoming obstacles and achieving success.

- **Family and Community Values:** The legacy of persistence is often embedded in the values and traditions of families and communities. Through the example of parents, elders, and community leaders who demonstrate persistence in their daily lives, younger generations learn the importance of perseverance, hard work, and determination in achieving their goals and contributing to their communities.

- **Legacy of Service and Giving Back:** The legacy of persistence is also reflected in the acts of service and philanthropy carried out by individuals who have achieved success through persistence. Many choose to give back to their communities, mentor others, or support causes that are dear to them, leaving behind a legacy of generosity, compassion, and social responsibility.

In essence, the legacy of persistence is a testament to the enduring power of human determination, resilience, and perseverance. It serves as a source of inspiration, motivation, and guidance for individuals and communities striving to overcome obstacles, achieve their goals, and leave a lasting impact on the world

CHAPTER 17

Conclusion: Embracing Persistence as a Lifelong Journey

In this final chapter, we reflect on the transformative power of persistence and its profound impact on our lives and the world around us. We emphasize that persistence is not just a trait but a lifelong journey—a commitment to continually strive for excellence, overcome obstacles, and pursue our dreams with unwavering determination. By embracing persistence as a way of life, we can navigate life's challenges with courage, grace, and resilience, knowing that with persistence as our compass, anything is possible. Let us embark on this journey of self-discovery and growth, embracing persistence as our greatest ally in the pursuit of a life filled with purpose, passion, and fulfillment.

Embracing persistence as a lifelong journey involves recognizing that the pursuit of goals, growth, and fulfillment is an ongoing process that requires dedication, resilience, and commitment. Here are some key aspects of embracing persistence as a lifelong journey:

- **Continuous Growth and Learning:** View persistence as a lifelong commitment to continuous growth and learning. Recognize that personal development is a journey that unfolds over time, and embrace opportunities for self-improvement, exploration, and discovery throughout life.

- **Adaptability and Flexibility:** Embrace the need to adapt and adjust your goals, plans, and strategies as circumstances change and new opportunities or challenges arise. Cultivate flexibility in your approach, and be willing to pivot, innovate, and explore new paths as you navigate your journey.

- **Resilience in the Face of Setbacks:** Understand that setbacks and obstacles are inevitable parts of any journey. Embrace resilience as a key trait that enables you to bounce back from setbacks, learn from failures, and persist in pursuit of your goals, even in the face of adversity.

- **Consistent Effort and Commitment:** Embrace the importance of consistent effort and commitment in achieving long-term success. Understand that progress often requires sustained dedication and perseverance over time, and be willing to invest the time, energy, and resources needed to realize your aspirations.

- **Celebrating Progress and Milestones:** Acknowledge and celebrate the progress you make along your journey, no matter how small or incremental. Take time to reflect on your achievements, milestones, and growth experiences, and use them as motivation to continue moving forward.

- **Staying True to Your Values:** Embrace persistence as a means of staying true to your values, passions, and purpose in life. Let your core beliefs and aspirations guide your journey and strive to align your actions with what matters most to you, even when faced with challenges or temptations to stray from your path.

- **Cultivating Supportive Relationships:** Surround yourself with supportive relationships and communities that encourage and empower you to pursue your goals and dreams. Seek out mentors, friends, and allies who believe in your potential and can provide guidance, encouragement, and accountability along your journey.

- **Embracing the Process:** Embrace the process of growth and transformation as an integral part of your journey. Understand that success is not just about reaching the destination, but also about embracing the journey itself— the lessons learned, the experiences gained, and the personal growth that occurs along the way.

- **Fostering a Positive Mindset:** Cultivate a positive mindset that focuses on possibilities, opportunities, and solutions, rather than dwelling on obstacles or limitations. Embrace optimism, resilience, and a can-do attitude as you navigate the ups and downs of your lifelong journey.

- **Embracing the Journey with Gratitude**: Finally, embrace your lifelong journey with a sense of gratitude for the opportunities, experiences, and connections that enrich your life along the way. Cultivate an attitude of gratitude for the blessings and lessons that each day brings and let gratitude fuel your persistence as you continue to grow, learn, and evolve on your journey.

- Here is Avtar Garcha wishing you every success in life. Stay Blessed. Amen

Made in the USA
Las Vegas, NV
10 July 2024

92133993R00039